KENSINGTON & CHELSEA
LIBRARIES

WITHDRAWN
FROM STOCK

FOR S
AS

D1141501

3 0116 02029070 4

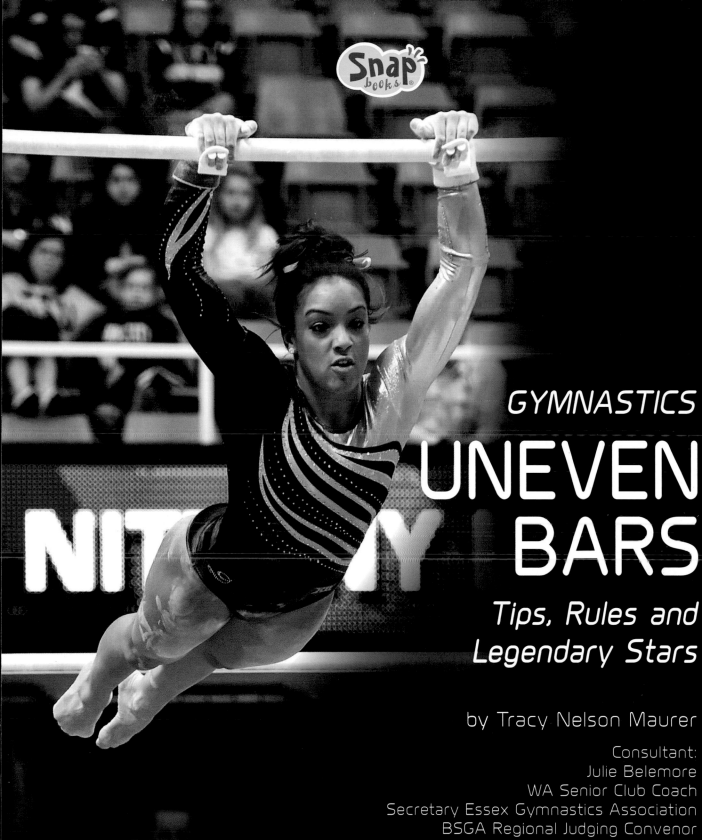

GYMNASTICS

UNEVEN BARS

Tips, Rules and Legendary Stars

by Tracy Nelson Maurer

Consultant:
Julie Belemore
WA Senior Club Coach
Secretary Essex Gymnastics Association
BSGA Regional Judging Convenor

Raintree is an imprint of Capstone Global Library Limited, a company incorporated in England and Wales having its registered office at 264 Banbury Road, Oxford, OX2 7DY – Registered company number: 6695582

www.raintree.co.uk
myorders@raintree.co.uk

Text © Capstone Global Library Limited 2017
The moral rights of the proprietor have been asserted.

All rights reserved. No part of this publication may be reproduced in any form or by any means (including photocopying or storing it in any medium by electronic means and whether or not transiently or incidentally to some other use of this publication) without the written permission of the copyright owner, except in accordance with the provisions of the Copyright, Designs and Patents Act 1988 or under the terms of a licence issued by the Copyright Licensing Agency, Saffron House, 6–10 Kirby Street, London EC1N 8TS (www.cla.co.uk). Applications for the copyright owner's written permission should be addressed to the publisher.

Edited by Gena Chester
Designed by Bobbie Nuytten
Picture research by Kelly Garvin
Production by Tori Abraham
Printed in China.

ISBN 978 1 4747 2633 7
20 19 18 17 16
10 9 8 7 6 5 4 3 2 1

British Library Cataloguing in Publication Data
A full catalogue record for this book is available from the British Library.

Acknowledgements
We would like to thank the following for permission to reproduce photographs: Capstone Press, Karon Dubke, 6, 7, 11, 12, 13, 14, 15, 19, 23, 25 (top), Martin Bustamante, 15, 17; Dreamstime/Ukrphoto, 5, 16; Getty Images, John Dominis/The LIFE Picture Collection, 26, Pascal Rondeau/Allsport, 28; Glow/Peter Muller, cover, 8; Newscom: Alan Edwards/Actionplus, 29, Geoff Burke/USA Today Sports, 24, Keystone Pictures USA/Zuma Press, 27; Shutterstock: Alex Emanuel Koch, 10, Aspen Photo, 1, Brendan Howard, 21, Fotos593, 25 (bottom), ID1974, 22, prapass, 23, Volt Collection, 9; Artistic Elements: Shutterstock: alexdndz, Bojanovic, Hakki Arslan

Every effort has been made to contact copyright holders of material reproduced in this book. Any omissions will be rectified in subsequent printings if notice is given to the publisher.

All the internet addresses (URLs) given in this book were valid at the time of going to press. However, due to the dynamic nature of the internet, some addresses may have changed, or sites may have changed or ceased to exist since publication. While the author and publisher regret any inconvenience this may cause readers, no responsibility for any such changes can be accepted by either the author or the publisher.

Contents

Take a swing
on the uneven bars

Imagine springing up to the lower uneven bar and holding on to it for a beat. You release and let your momentum swing you into the next move. You fly fluidly between the lower and upper bar with airborne skills. One final flip, and you stick your landing.

Routines on the uneven bar **apparatus** are thrilling to watch. They show a gymnast's strength, endurance and flair. Each routine features moves that flow from one to the next. The entire performance lasts for about 45 seconds. But it takes months and even years of hard practise to polish every detail.

Only women gymnasts compete on the uneven bars and balance beam. Men compete on the parallel bars, the horizontal bar, pommel horse and rings. All gymnasts compete in the vault and floor exercise events. These events are all part of artistic gymnastics.

Fast fact:
Artistic gymnastics appeared in the first Olympic Games in 1896 in Athens. Men's rope climbing, parallel bars and horizontal bar were some of the artistic gymnastics events in 1896.

apparatus equipment used in gymnastics, such as the uneven bars

Chapter 1

Get fit, get ready

Gymnastics clubs are the easiest, safest and most efficient way to learn the sport. British Gymnastics sets rules and standards for clubs and competitions. Go to British Gymnastics' official website for a list of member clubs near you.

You will need to work hard before you first grip the uneven bars. Coaches help gymnasts build physical fitness for strength and body control. A gymnast on the uneven bars must be able to hold her own body weight. Chin-ups, pull-ups and push-ups are common exercises – and that's just for starters! Conditioning at training sessions may also include core exercises, such as sit-ups, planks and leg lifts. **Aerobic exercises**, such as star jumps, are essential for building strength and **stamina**. Muscle stretches occur before and after practices to build flexibility and grace.

Exercising outside of the gym is time well spent. Practise handstands and do sit ups at home. They can help build the balance and strength necessary for skills attempted in the gym. But save your actual uneven bar skills for the gym. There a coach can make sure you're performing moves correctly and safely.

aerobic exercise activity that works the heart and lungs

stamina energy and strength to keep doing something for a long period of time

Changing apparatus

Uneven bar gymnasts learn basic skills on a single, low bar. They add the second bar as they build skills and gain confidence.

The bar height can be adjusted for all but the top competitors. Beginners should use a bar set at chest height. Advanced gymnasts must use the apparatus with the lower bar 1.7 metres (5.5 feet) above the floor. The upper bar must stand at 2.5 metres (8.2 feet) or higher from the floor.

The distance between the bars gives gymnasts room to perform skills. In the early days of the event, the bars were set about shoulder-width apart. Routines then focused on swinging moves, simple rotations around the bars, and handstands or holds. As gymnasts added more difficult skills, they needed more space between the bars. Today the two bars are spread about 1.8 metres (6 feet) apart.

Fast fact:

Uneven bars first appeared at an international competition in 1934 at the Artistic Gymnastics World Championships in Budapest. This was also the first women's World Championships.

Better bars

Until the 1960s, uneven bars were oval shaped and made of wood. They sometimes broke during routines. Today bars are made of **fibreglass** with wood around it. Bars are round so they're easier to grip. Anchor cables also make the apparatus safer by providing extra support.

Safety first!

Falls are common, especially as you learn new moves on the uneven bars. Mats on the floor cushion falls. Injuries can be avoided by falling safely. Land on the mat with your arms tucked in, never outstretched or reaching behind your body. Always work out on the uneven bars with a coach near the apparatus ready to help you.

fibreglass strong, lightweight material made from thin threads of glass

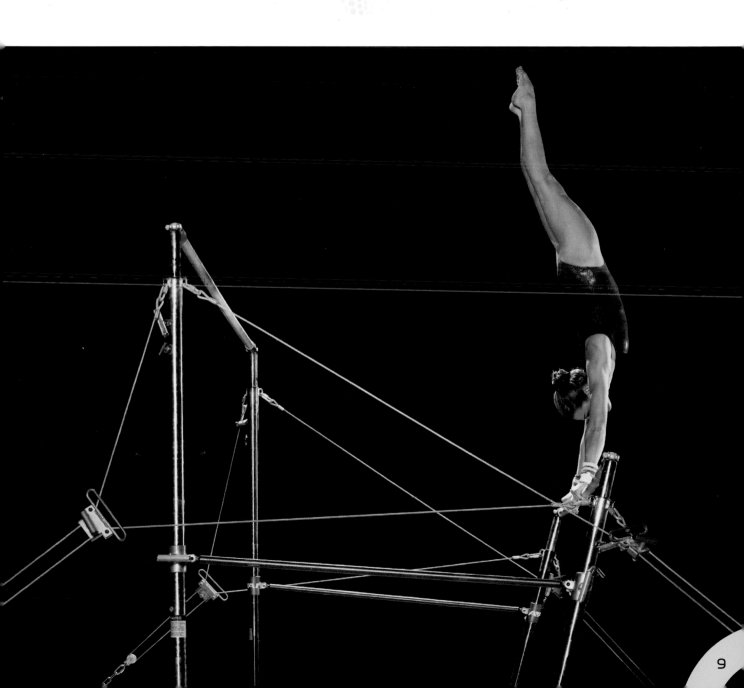

Practice and performance gear

Gymnasts come to the gym ready to train. They wear stretchy, close-fitting clothing to prevent fabric from catching on the bars and causing accidents.

At competitions gymnasts wear **leotards**. Team members must wear matching leotards. They wear tracksuits before and after performing to keep their muscles warm.

Many gymnasts wear braces called handguards on both hands to help prevent painful blisters from forming when their palms rub against the bar. Handguards help keep their hands from slipping off the bar too.

Each handguard has a leather strip from the wrist to the fingertips. The middle and fourth fingertips slip into two holes in the strip. The guard wraps tightly at the wrist. Chalk is added to hands and the grips to absorb sweat. Most gymnasts also wear wristbands under the guards to absorb more sweat. A small wooden dowel, under the leather at the fingertips, can be added for extra gripping power.

leotard snug, one-piece garment worn by gymnasts and dancers

Chapter 2

Get a
grip

Working the uneven bars requires a strong grip, but not just any grip. Every move uses a certain grip position. Grips can either provide stability or add difficulty to a move. They help the routine flow smoothly from skill to skill.

Judges at competitions check grip positions. They also look for powerful releases. A release is when a gymnast lets go of the bar for a skill and then grabs it again.

Grip positions

Over or regular grip

Knuckles face up, palms face away

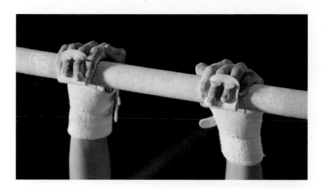

Under or reverse grip

Knuckles face away, palms face you

Mixed grip

One over and one under grip

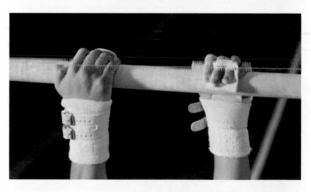

Eagle, L or dorsal grip

Arms rotated with elbows facing forward, hands in an over grip with thumbs pointed away from the body

Each bar routine has three phases: the **mount** onto the bars, a series of skills and the **dismount**. Judges score every element of each phase.

Phase 1: the mount

The mount sets the routine in motion. Beginners can simply hop up and grab the low bar. Part of the mount is getting into position for the first element. A gymnast may start by pulling the body up and over the bar for an upward cycle. They might also start by hanging in basic positions, such as a pike, straddle or tuck.

Gymnasts add difficulty to the mount with an upstart, which is a move that helps a gymnast gain momentum. Do you remember pumping a swing at the playground to fly higher? The float upstart works the same way. It helps position the body for the next skill and connects skills together.

Advanced gymnasts may choose to use a **springboard** to **somersault** or twist onto the bars. Some athletes leapfrog the low bar to reach the high bar!

a pullover

mount move done to get on to an apparatus
dismount move done to get off of an apparatus
springboard strong, flexible board that is used for jumping very high
somersault gymnastics move where you tuck your head into your chest and roll in a circle

Basic hangs

Shoulders stay below the bar and arms hang straight from the bar.

Pike

Bend at the hips, legs stretched out straight

Tuck

Tuck both legs up to the chest

Straddle

Make a "V" with straight legs

The float upstart

1. From the floor or a springboard, jump with your arms reaching for the low bar. Use an over grip to hang from the bar as your body glides and extends under the bar with your legs straight in a pike or straddle position.

2. Lift your toes up to the bar and swing back.

3. Use the swing's energy to pull your body up as you push down on the bar. Keep your arms straight. Bring your hips to the bar into a front support. Look straight ahead.

Phase 2: the routine

This is where the high-flying action takes off! Gymnasts push the difficulty levels of skills with awesome results.

Elite gymnasts compete using rules set by the Fédération Internationale de Gymnastique (FIG). The rules are listed in the official rule book called the Code of Points. British Gymnastics also uses their Women's Artistic Gymnastics Competition Handbook in their sponsored competitions. The required elements in an elite routine come from five groups:

1. casts, also called layaways

2. forward and backward giant swings that make a complete rotation around the bar and end in a handstand

3. circle swings, including hips and shoulders swinging around the bar in a pike or straddle from one handstand into another

4. release moves

5. dismounts

elite describes gymnasts who are among the best

The back hip circle

Remember to keep your arms straight.

1. First do a cast, a pump for momentum to launch the rotation. Move your legs forward then backward and up as you push down on the bar.

2. Bring your hips back to the bar. Lean your shoulders back as your legs move forward under the bar.

3. Angle your legs about 45 degrees and spin around the bar in a full circle.

Fast fact:
If a gymnast falls in competition, she has 30 seconds to chalk her hands and remount to start again.

Phase 3: the dismount

The last phase of a routine is often the most exciting to watch. The suspense felt by the audience reaches its peak when a gymnast lands her dismount perfectly.

Beginner gymansts release the bar and add flair to their landing with an underswing or a sole circle. Advanced gymnasts spin, flip or twist in daring moves down from the bars.

The triple back tuck, or Magaña, ranks as one of the most difficult dismounts. It requires three tucked rotations from the high bar. It's rarely attempted in competitions.

All gymnasts try to stick their landings. Wobbles or steps backward or forward lower the score. According to the FIG Code of Points, failure to land feet first is a minimum 1.00 point deduction.

Fast fact:
Brenda Magaña Almaral of Mexico was the first to land the triple back tuck in 2002.

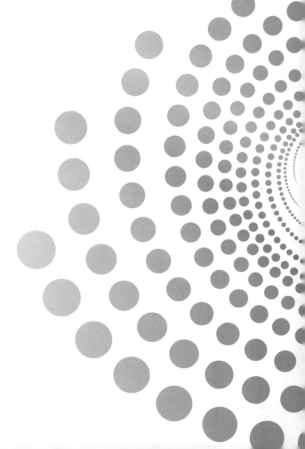

Chapter 3

Meet to compete

Practices, workouts, bruises and sore muscles all come together in less than a minute at a competition. Members of British Gymnastics can compete at county, regional and national levels.

The highest level in British Gymnastics is called Compulsory Elite Grades. Gymnasts compete on uneven bars, vault, balance beam and floor, as well as a range and conditioning program. Within the Elite Grades, gymnasts move from level 5 (lowest) to level 1 (highest). Moving up to the next level depends on age and mastery of skills.

For the uneven bar, **compulsory** levels must perform a set routine. Routines are specific to each level. Gymnasts perform routines on just one bar until Level 1.

Compulsory level 5 gymnasts are eight years old. Compulsory level 1 gymnasts are at least 12 years old. The top competitors for levels 4–1 may be selected to join national competitions, such as the British Espoir. The decision is based on the gymnasts' performances at regional and voluntary competitions.

Fast fact:
Gymnasts in the Elite Grades usually train from 30 to 40 hours a week.

compulsory required element or routine

British Gymnastics offers less competitive programs for every type of gymnast. Programs under the Gymnastics for All discipline focus on fun and fitness. Almost anyone regardless of age and skill can participate. In the program they learn a variety of elements from catagories like artistic and rythmic gymnastics, sports acrobatics and trampoline.

an artistic gymnastics competition in Moscow, Russia

A major gymnastics competition fills an arena with families, friends, and fans. Vault, uneven bars, balance beam, and floor exercises often happen at the same time in the same gymnasium. Music from the floor exercise blares over cheers for uneven bar tricks. The atmosphere is noisy and exciting.

Each event has compulsory skills that show gymnasts' abilities, creativity, and style. These skills are combined to form elements to make up a routine. Depending on the competition, two to eight judges evaluate each routine. Elite gymnasts hope for high 15s and 16s. But it's possible to score above 17.

Individual gymnasts can win medals in a single event, such as the uneven bars, or for all-around. The best scores combined from all of the events determine all-around medals. Gymnasts can also win medals as a team.

Code of Points

Difficulty – D Score

Every element in a routine is separated and scored. It is then assigned a point value based on difficulty. The easiest element, or A, has a value of 0.1. Difficulty increases with each letter. After A, the next highest difficulty is B. For each additional letter there is an increase of 0.1 in points. Judges also give "connection" points for linking the top elements in a performance. The gymnast receives 0.50 points for each completed requirement as well.

Execution – E Score

Each judge starts at 10. They subtract 0.1 for tiny mistakes and up to a whole point for large mistakes, such as a fall. The highest and lowest scores from the judges are taken out. The average of the remaining scores is the E score. Once both the D and E scores are determined, they are added together for one final score.

Fast fact:

Four gymnasts tied for gold in the uneven bars at the 2015 World Championships. The four-way tie was a historic first for the Championships. Viktoria Komova and Daria Spiridonova of Russia earned a winning score of 15.366. Fan Yilin of China and Madison Kocian of the United States scored the exact same number to win as well.

Gymnasts want to look strong and confident performing their tricks on the uneven bars. They also want to emphasize their unique style through their appearance.

Hairstyles must keep hair from the face. Gymnasts might have short haircuts with a short fringe or long hair tied back with a few small plaits in a bun, ponytail or bunches. Most gymnasts match their leotards to their hair bands. Hair grips, butterfly clips and loads of gel and hairspray keep hair-dos in place.

Some older gymnasts add to their look with makeup. Brazilian gymnast Daniele Hypolito wore vibrant green, yellow and blue eyeshadow at the 2012 Olympics. Many gymnasts wear eyeliner and waterproof mascara. A few wear glitter around their eyes or in their hair. Some wear bold lip stain for colour. Others go for a more natural look with neutral colours and clear lip gloss.

Daniele Hypolito's eyeshadow matched Brazil's national colours.

Your gym bag packing list

Pack your bag the night before a competition.
This will save you time and stress.

- water bottle
- towel
- handguards
- chalk powder
- makeup
- hairbrush, clips, ties and hair products
- gym slippers if you don't perform
  in bare feet

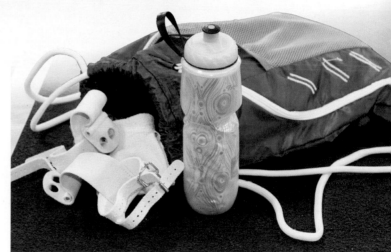

Chapter 4

Legends of the uneven bars

From attempting the hardest moves to inventing new ones, some athletes have left a lasting impression on the uneven bars event. Their athleticism and grace has influenced the way we see gymnastics today, and their stories of success inspire young gymnasts around the world.

Olga Korbut

Olga Korbut shook up the gymnastics world in 1972 during the Olympic events. At 17 years old, Olga competed in the balance beam, floor, and uneven bars events as the youngest person on the team for the Soviet Union. She won three gold medals and one silver medal.

During the uneven bars event, Olga performed an aerial backward somersault from a standing position on the high bar. She was the first gymnast ever to perform this move at the Olympics. It was later named the Korbut Flip in the FIG Code of Points. During the routine, she also nailed a back flip from the low bar to the high bar. The audience loved it! When the judges gave her only a 9.8 out of 10 points, fans yelled and stomped their feet. Today moves from the feet, such as the Korbut Flip, are banned from competition.

Nadia Comaneci

At 14 years old, Nadia Comaneci represented Romania in the uneven bars event at the 1976 Olympic Games. She was the first Olympic gymnast to receive a perfect score, which was 10 points then. But the scoreboard wasn't designed to show 10. Her score came up as 1.0. It confused the crowd at first.

Nadia earned seven perfect scores at the 1976 Games, winning three gold medals for the uneven bars, balance beam, and individual all-around. She also won a bronze medal and a team silver medal. Nadia won two more gold and silver medals at the 1980 Olympic Games.

The Comaneci Salto

The Comaneci Salto is a move named after gymnast Nadia Comaneci. It starts from a front support. The gymnast casts and pushes away from the bar. Then she flips forward for the Salto in a straddle position and catches the bar in a hang.

Fast fact:
When a gymnast invents a new skill, it must be performed at a World Gymnastics Championship or Olympics competition to be named after him or her in the FIG Code of Points.

Shannon Miller

As a baby, Shannon Miller wore a brace attached to her feet to keep her legs from growing inward. She overcame this first challenge with the same determination that helped her become an elite gymnast. In the 1992 Olympics Games, she represented the United States in the balance beam, floor exercise, and uneven bars events. Shannon was the first American to win five gold medals in any sport at the Olympic Games.

Shannon competed in 1996 with the "Magnificent Seven" Olympic team that earned the US gymnastics team its first team gold medal. She has seven Olympic medals and nine World Championship medals. She's the only woman in any sport to be inducted into the United States Olympic Hall of Fame twice, as an individual and as part of a team.

Fast fact:

The Code of Points includes two skills with Shannon's name on them. The Miller features a cast to a handstand, followed by a one-and-a-half turn to a mixed-L grip on the uneven bars.

Elizabeth 'Beth' Tweddle

Great Britain's greatest gymnast of all time, Elizabeth 'Beth' Tweddle chose gymnastics when she was seven years old after trying several other sports. She competed in her first World Championships in 2001. The next year, she placed third on the uneven bars at the European Championships. No other British female gymnast had ever earned a medal at this competition!

Beth went on to win more than 20 international medals, including the 2012 Olympic bronze medal for the uneven bars. She holds three World Championship titles, six European titles and a World Cup Final. She's best known for her bold floor exercises and daring uneven bar routines. The Queen of England awarded Beth a Member of the Order of the British Empire (MBE) in 2010, Britain's highest recognition for her service to the sport.

As with other sports, there are no shortcuts to success in gymnastics. Winning a 45-second uneven bars routine takes a great deal of practise. But it's easy to find gymnasts around the world who are willing to give their all to the sport.

Glossary

aerobic exercise activity that works the heart and lungs

apparatus equipment used in gymnastics, such as the uneven bars

compulsory required element or routine

dismount move done to get off of an apparatus

elite describes gymnasts who are among the best

fibreglass strong, lightweight material made from thin threads of glass

leotard snug, one-piece garment worn by gymnasts and dancers

mount move done to get on to an apparatus

springboard strong, flexible board that is used for jumping very high

somersault gymnastics move where you tuck your head into your chest and roll in a circle

stamina energy and strength to keep doing something for a long period of time

Read more

Gymnastics (Mad about), J. Heneghan (Wayland, 2016)

The Science Behind Gymnastics (Science of the Summer Olympics), L.E. Carmichael (Raintree, 2016)

Becoming an Olympic Gymnast (Collins Big Cat), Beth Tweddle (Collins Educational, 2012)

Websites

www.british-gymnastics.org
Find a club near where you live and take a look at the profiles of your favourite British gymnasts.

www.fig-gymnastics.com
Look at all of the official rules of gymnastics at the official website of the Fédération Internationale de Gymnastique.

www.ukgymnastics.org
Find out all the latest news about gymnastics in the United Kingdom.

INDEX